THE BEST WAY TO IMPROVE ON COMMUNICATION SKILLS

Unlock The Secrets Of Active Listening For Deeper Connections

Nick Evans Brown

NICK EVANS BROWN

Copyright©2024 Nick Evans Brown

All Rights Reserve

YOU CAN GET ACCESS TO MORE BOOKS HERE:

OR

USING THE LINK BELOW:

https://amzn.to/3OvHJcr

THE BEST WAY TO IMPROVE ON COMMUNICATION SKILLS

TABLE OF CONTENT

INTRODUCTION

CHAPTER ONE

1.0 THE FOUNDATION OF ACTIVE LISTENING

1.1 TRANSFORMING CONVERSATIONS THROUGH ACTIVE LISTENING

1.2 COMMON BARRIERS TO ACTIVE LISTENING

CHAPTER TWO

2.0 THE POWER OF NON-VERBAL COMMUNICATION

2.1 THE ROLE OF NON-VERBAL COMMUNICATION IN RELATIONSHIPS

2.2 THE INTERPLAY BETWEEN NON-VERBAL CUES

2.3 THE IMPORTANCE OF CULTURAL DIFFERENCES IN INTERPRETING NON-VERBAL CUES

CHAPTER THREE

3.0 ADAPTING YOUR COMMUNICATION STYLE

3.1 STRATEGIES FOR IDENTIFYING YOUR OWN STYLE

3.2 THE POWER OF STORYTELLING

CONCLUSION

THE BEST WAY TO IMPROVE ON COMMUNICATION SKILLS

INTRODUCTION

Being able to really listen can set you apart in a world where talking to people is more important than ever. Here's "The Best Way to Improve on Communication Skills: Unlock the Secrets of Active Listening for Deeper Connections."

This book is meant to help you learn the transformative art of active listening, which will not only make your talks better but also help you make deeper, more meaningful connections at work and in your personal life.

Did you know that bad communication is the cause of almost 70% of mistakes at work? Misunderstandings in relationships often happen because people don't listen well. These numbers show that we need to improve the way we talk to each other right away. You can avoid arguments, build trust, and make a space where everyone feels

THE BEST WAY TO IMPROVE ON COMMUNICATION SKILLS

heard and respected by improving your active listening skills.

You will go on a trip through this book to find out how to do active listening. We'll start by talking about what "active listening" really means and how it can change the way you talk to people in Chapter 1. Chapter 2 will delve into the power of non-verbal communication, showing how body language and tone can enhance your message. Finally, in Chapter 3, you'll learn how to adapt your communication style to connect with diverse audiences successfully.

Each chapter is packed with actionable insights and practical techniques that you can apply right away. By the end of this book, you'll not only understand the importance of active listening but also possess the tools to change your conversations and relationships for the better. Let's get started on this

NICK EVANS BROWN

exciting journey toward becoming a more effective speaker!

THE BEST WAY TO IMPROVE ON COMMUNICATION SKILLS

CHAPTER ONE

1.0 The Foundation of Active Listening

"Most people do not listen with the intent to understand; they listen with the intent to reply." — Covey, Stephen R.

A common mistake in communication is putting our own thoughts and reactions ahead of really listening to what others are saying. This powerful quote captures this tendency. In a time when information is shared instantly, careful listening has never been more important. Not only hearing words, but also understanding, processing, and reacting carefully to what someone is saying.

Read this chapter to learn about the basics of active hearing, why it's important for good communication, and how mastering this skill can change the way we talk to each other and make our relationships stronger.

THE BEST WAY TO IMPROVE ON COMMUNICATION SKILLS

Understanding Active Listening

Active listening means making a conscious effort to fully engage with a speaker, understand what they are saying, and react in the right way. Active listening, on the other hand, takes focus and participation. With passive listening, you might just hear words without really thinking about what they mean. It has several important parts:

Attention: The viewer must pay full attention to the speaker, setting aside distractions and personal thoughts.

Understanding: This includes comprehending both the content of the message and the emotions behind it.

Feedback: Providing appropriate responses that show understanding and engagement.

Significance in Effective Communication

The significance of active listening in successful conversation cannot be overstated. It serves as a cornerstone for building trust and rapport in relationships, whether personal or business. Here are several ways that learning active listening can transform conversations:

Enhancing Clarity: Active listening allows listeners to explain ambiguities and ensure that both parties are aligned. By asking questions or paraphrasing what has been said, listeners can confirm their knowledge and reduce the likelihood of misunderstandings.

Fostering Collaboration: In work settings, active listening encourages collaboration among team members. When individuals feel heard, they are more likely to contribute ideas and participate in constructive dialogue, leading to better outcomes.

THE BEST WAY TO IMPROVE ON COMMUNICATION SKILLS

Strengthening Relationships: Personal relationships grow on mutual understanding and empathy. Active listening allows individuals to connect on a deeper emotional level, fostering intimacy and trust. When people feel that their thoughts and feelings are valued, they are more likely to open up and share genuinely.

Psychological Benefits Of Active Listening

Beyond improving communication, active listening offers deep psychological benefits:

Increased Empathy: Engaging deeply with another person's viewpoint fosters empathy, allowing us to connect with others on a human level. This connection improves our ability to understand their feelings and viewpoints.

Reduced Misunderstandings: Active listeners are less likely to misinterpret messages because they take the time to clarify and think on what has been said. This leads to clearer conversation and fewer conflicts.

Enhanced Emotional Regulation: By focusing on the speaker's message rather than their reactions, listeners can maintain composure during challenging talks. This helps in managing emotions effectively, reducing stress for both parties concerned.

1.1 Transforming Conversations Through Active Listening

Mastering active listening can lead to profound transformations in how we interact with others. Here's how it can change talks for the better:

Creating Safe Spaces: When we practice active listening, we create a setting where speakers feel safe expressing themselves without fear of Judgment Or Interruption. This fosters open dialogue and honest expression.

THE BEST WAY TO IMPROVE ON COMMUNICATION SKILLS

Building Trust: Trust is built through the constant practice of active listening. When individuals feel heard and understood, they are more likely to trust their listeners, leading to better relationships both personally and professionally.

Encouraging Deeper Connections: Active listening allows for deeper connections by allowing individuals to share their thoughts and feelings more freely. This emotional exchange promotes intimacy and strengthens bonds between people.

Facilitating Conflict Resolution: In situations of disagreement or conflict, active listening plays a critical part in finding common ground. By genuinely trying to understand differing perspectives, people can navigate conflicts more effectively.

Promoting Personal Growth: Engaging with different viewpoints through active listening broadens our understanding of the world around us. It encourages us to think on our beliefs and consider alternative viewpoints, fostering personal growth.

Active listening is not merely a passive activity; it is a conscious practice that requires effort and commitment. By understanding its significance in successful communication and implementing key techniques such as being fully present, using positive body language, and providing thoughtful feedback, people can transform their conversations into meaningful exchanges that foster deeper connections.

As we continue exploring active listening throughout this book, remember that each interaction presents a chance for growth—not only in how we communicate but also in how we connect with those around us. By committing to becoming better listeners, we pave the way for richer relationships and more fulfilling interactions in every part of our lives.

THE BEST WAY TO IMPROVE ON COMMUNICATION SKILLS

In summary, active listening is a critical skill that improves our ability to communicate effectively while fostering empathy and understanding among individuals. By recognizing its importance and actively practicing it in our daily interactions, we can greatly improve our relationships both personally and professionally.

Key Techniques For Active Listening

Active listening is a vital skill that improves communication and promotes deeper connections. It includes fully engaging with the speaker, understanding their message, and responding thoughtfully. This chapter will cover three key techniques for active listening: being fully present, using positive body language, and paraphrasing and reflecting. Each of these methods plays a crucial role in ensuring effective communication and building meaningful relationships.

Be Fully Present

Being fully present is the cornerstone of active listening. It means giving the speaker your full attention and minimizing distractions to focus entirely on what they are saying. Here are several practical methods to achieve this:

1. Minimize Distractions

Distractions can significantly hinder your ability to listen effectively. To build an environment conducive to active listening, consider the following:

Choose the Right Setting: Find a quiet place where interruptions are minimized. This could be a private office, a quiet café, or even a secluded place in a park.

Turn Off Notifications: Silence your phone, close your laptop, and put away any other devices that might divert your attention during the talk.

THE BEST WAY TO IMPROVE ON COMMUNICATION SKILLS

Clear Your thoughts: Before engaging in a conversation, take a moment to clear your thoughts of distractions. Focus on the present moment and set aside any personal worries or thoughts that might interfere with your ability to listen.

2. Maintain Eye Contact

Eye contact is a powerful non-verbal cue that suggests attentiveness and interest. When you keep eye contact with the speaker, you convey that you are engaged in the conversation and value their input. Here are some tips for successful eye contact:

Be Mindful of Cultural Differences: While maintaining eye contact is usually a sign of attentiveness in many cultures, it may be perceived differently in others. Be aware of national norms regarding eye contact to ensure you are not unintentionally making the speaker uncomfortable.

Use Eye Contact Appropriately: Aim for natural eye contact—avoid staring, as this can be frightening. Instead, keep eye contact intermittently while also allowing for brief breaks to avoid discomfort.

3. Listen Without Preparing Your Response

One of the most common barriers to active listening is the desire to formulate a response while the other person is speaking. This not only distracts you from getting their message but also prevents you from fully engaging with their thoughts. To prevent this habit:

Focus on Understanding: Concentrate on what the speaker is saying rather than thinking about how you will react. Allow yourself to absorb their words fully before considering your reply.

Practice Patience: Allow for pauses in the talk. Sometimes, speakers need time to gather their thoughts or expand on their points. Resist the desire to fill the silence with your comments.

THE BEST WAY TO IMPROVE ON COMMUNICATION SKILLS

Use Positive Body Language

Non-verbal communication plays a critical part in active listening. Your body language can communicate attentiveness and openness, enhancing the effectiveness of your interactions. Here are some key features of positive body language:

1. Show Engagement Through Gestures

Your gestures can express attention and encouragement without interrupting the speaker's flow:

Nod Occasionally: Nodding your head at appropriate moments shows that you are following along and encourages the speaker to continue.

Facial Expressions: Use facial expressions that show empathy or interest based on what is being discussed. A smile can convey warmth, while a concerned look can show that you care about their feelings.

Maintain an Open Posture: Avoid crossing your arms or legs, as this can signal defensiveness or boredom. Instead, adopt an open stance by facing the speaker directly with relaxed arms.

2. Use Verbal Affirmations

In addition to non-verbal cues, verbal affirmations can improve communication by showing that you are engaged:

Encourage with Small Comments: Use brief vocal affirmations like "Yes," "I see," or "Go on" to encourage the speaker to continue sharing their thoughts.

recognize Emotions: If the speaker expresses strong feelings, recognize them directly by saying things like "That sounds challenging" or "I can see how that would make you feel upset." This validates their emotions and fosters connection.

THE BEST WAY TO IMPROVE ON COMMUNICATION SKILLS

Paraphrase And Reflect

Paraphrasing and reflecting are important techniques in active listening that show engagement and confirm understanding.

1. Summarize What Has Been Said

Paraphrasing involves restating what the speaker has said in your own words. This method serves multiple purposes:

Confirm Understanding: By summarizing key points, you ensure that you have properly understood the speaker's message. For example, you might say, "What I'm hearing is that you're feeling overwhelmed by your workload."

Encourage Further Discussion: Paraphrasing asks the speaker to elaborate on their ideas or clarify any misunderstandings. It shows that you are invested in their view.

2. Ask Clarifying Questions

Asking questions is another effective way to connect with the speaker's message:

Seek Clarification: If something is unclear, don't fear to ask questions like "What do you mean when you say...?" or "Can you elaborate on that point?" This demonstrates your desire to understand fully.

Explore Feelings: In addition to clarifying content, consider asking about feelings connected with what they are sharing. Questions like "How did that make you feel?" can deepen emotional connections.

Active listening is an important skill that enhances communication and fosters deeper connections between people. By being fully present, using positive body language, and practicing paraphrasing and reflecting methods, listeners can create an environment where speakers feel valued and understood.

THE BEST WAY TO IMPROVE ON COMMUNICATION SKILLS

Implementing these techniques takes practice and commitment but leads to significant improvements in communication effectiveness. As we continue our exploration of active listening throughout this book, remember that each interaction presents a chance for growth—not only in how we communicate but also in how we connect with those around us. By committing to becoming better listeners through these key techniques, we pave the way for richer relationships and more fulfilling interactions in every part of our lives.

Overcoming Barriers To Active Listening

Active listening is a critical skill that enhances communication and fosters deeper connections in both personal and professional settings. However, several hurdles can impede our ability to listen effectively. Understanding these barriers—such as preconceived ideas, emotional reactions, and environmental distractions—allows us to develop strategies for overcoming them. This chapter will identify these common barriers and provide actionable techniques to ensure that every talk is meaningful, from casual exchanges to critical discussions. Additionally, we will study mindfulness practices that can enhance our listening skills.

1.2 Common Barriers To Active Listening

1. Preconceived Notions

Preconceived notions are biases or assumptions we hold about a speaker or their message before the conversation even starts. These biases can come from past experiences, stereotypes, or personal beliefs. When we enter a conversation with preconceived ideas, we may filter the speaker's words through our biases, leading to misunderstandings or dismissive attitudes.

Example: If you think that a colleague is often negative, you might tune out their input during a meeting, assuming it will be unhelpful without fully hearing their ideas.

THE BEST WAY TO IMPROVE ON COMMUNICATION SKILLS

2. Emotional Reactions

Emotions can greatly impact our ability to listen actively. Strong feelings—whether positive or negative—can cloud our judgment and lead us to respond impulsively rather than thoughtfully. For instance, if someone criticizes your work, you might feel defensive and stop hearing altogether.

Example: During a performance review, if your manager suggests an area for improvement, you may become anxious or upset, making it difficult to absorb constructive feedback.

3. Environmental Distractions

Environmental distractions include any external factors that disrupt our attention during a conversation. This can range from background noise and interruptions to awkward settings. Such distractions can make it challenging to focus on the speaker's message.

Example: Trying to have an important talk in a noisy café or while multiple conversations are happening around you can hinder your ability to listen effectively.

Actionable Techniques For Overcoming Barriers

To enhance active listening skills and overcome these barriers, try implementing the following techniques:

1. Cultivate Self-Awareness

Self-awareness is the first step in overcoming obstacles to active listening. By recognizing your own biases and emotional triggers, you can control them more effectively during conversations.

Reflect on Your Biases: Before engaging in discussions, take a moment to consider any preconceived ideas you may have about the speaker or subject. Acknowledge these biases and set a goal to listen openly.

THE BEST WAY TO IMPROVE ON COMMUNICATION SKILLS

Identify Emotional Triggers: Be aware of your emotional reactions during conversations. If you notice yourself becoming defensive or upset, take a deep breath and remind yourself of the importance of understanding the speaker's viewpoint.

2. Create an Optimal Listening Environment

Minimizing environmental distractions is important for effective listening. Here are some real steps:

Choose the Right Location: Whenever possible, pick a quiet space for important conversations. Avoid places with loud background noise or frequent interruptions.

Limit Visual Distractions: Clear your workspace of items that might divert your attention during talks. This could mean closing useless tabs on your computer or putting away your phone.

Use Headphones: In open office settings or noisy environments, consider using noise-canceling headphones while engaged in conversations via phone or video calls.

3. Practice Mindfulness Techniques

Mindfulness practices can greatly enhance your ability to listen actively by helping you stay focused on the present moment:

Mindful Breathing: Before starting a conversation, take a few moments to practice deep breathing exercises. Inhale deeply through your nose for four counts, hold for four counts, and exit through your mouth for four counts. This can help calm your mind and prepare you for focused listening.

Grounding Exercises: Use grounding techniques to bring your awareness back to the present moment if you find your thoughts drifting during a talk. Focus on physical sensations—like feeling your feet on the ground or the texture of the chair you're sitting in—to stabilize yourself.

4. Employ Active Engagement Techniques

Engaging actively with the speaker not only helps you stay focused but also shows your commitment to understanding their message:

Ask Open-Ended Questions: Encourage deeper dialogue by asking questions that invite elaboration rather than easy yes-or-no answers. For example, instead of saying "Did you like the project?" try "What parts of the project did you find most valuable?"

Paraphrase and Reflect: Summarize what the speaker has said in your own words to confirm knowledge and show engagement. For example, "So what I'm hearing is that you felt overwhelmed by the deadlines last week."

Practice Empathy: Make an effort to understand the speaker's feelings and viewpoint by acknowledging their emotions. Use words like "I can see why that would be frustrating" or "It sounds like you're passionate about this topic."

1.3 Mindfulness Practices That Enhance Listening Capabilities

Mindfulness not only helps in managing distractions but also enhances general communication skills by fostering greater awareness of both yourself and others:

1. Develop Presence Through Mindfulness Meditation

Regular awareness meditation can train your mind to focus better during conversations:

Set Aside Time for Meditation: Spend just five minutes each day practicing mindfulness meditation by focusing on your breath and watching thoughts without judgment.

THE BEST WAY TO IMPROVE ON COMMUNICATION SKILLS

Body Scan Technique: Engage in body scan meditation where you mentally check in with different parts of your body while breathing deeply. This practice can increase body awareness and help reduce tension before participating in conversations.

2. Cultivate an Open Mindset

Approaching talks with an open mindset allows for greater receptivity:

Suspend Judgment: Remind yourself that every conversation is a chance to learn something new. Challenge yourself to set aside any preconceived opinions about what the speaker will say.

Practice Gratitude: Before engaging in discussions, take a moment to think on what you appreciate about the person you are speaking with or the insights they may offer. This mindset shift can promote openness and curiosity during conversations.

Overcoming barriers to active listening is important for effective communication and building meaningful connections with others. By identifying common barriers such as preconceived notions, emotional reactions, and environmental distractions, people can equip themselves with actionable techniques meant to enhance their listening skills.

Implementing strategies like cultivating self-awareness, building optimal listening environments, practicing mindfulness techniques, and employing active engagement methods will greatly improve one's ability to listen actively. As we continue our exploration of active listening throughout this book, remember that every conversation presents a chance for growth—not only in how we communicate but also in how we connect with those around us. By committing ourselves to overcoming these barriers, we open the way for richer

THE BEST WAY TO IMPROVE ON COMMUNICATION SKILLS

relationships and more fulfilling interactions across all parts of life.

CHAPTER TWO

2.0 The Power Of Non-Verbal Communication

"The most important thing in communication is hearing what isn't said." – Peter Drucker.

This insightful quote underscores the important role of non-verbal cues in understanding messages beyond spoken words. Non-verbal communication includes a wide array of signals, including body language, facial expressions, and tone of voice, all of which can significantly impact the effectiveness of our interactions.

In this chapter, we will delve into the various types of non-verbal communication, examine their impact on conversations, and highlight the importance of recognizing these cues to enhance our communication skills.

THE BEST WAY TO IMPROVE ON COMMUNICATION SKILLS

Understanding Non-Verbal Cues

Non-verbal communication refers to the transmission of ideas without the use of words. It includes several forms, each adding to how we convey and interpret meaning in our interactions.

Types Of Non-Verbal Communication

Body Language: This includes gestures, posture, and movements. Body language can suggest confidence, openness, or defensiveness. For example, standing tall with an open posture expresses confidence, while slouching may suggest insecurity or disinterest.

Facial Expressions: Our faces are highly expressive and can communicate a range of emotions—happiness, sadness, anger, surprise—without a single word being spoken. A smile can express warmth and friendliness, while a furrowed brow might suggest concern or disagreement.

Tone of Voice (Paralinguistics): The tone, pitch, volume, and pace of our speech can greatly alter the meaning of our words. For instance, a cheerful tone can improve a positive message, while a flat tone may suggest disinterest or sarcasm.

Eye Contact: Eye contact plays a crucial part in establishing trust and connection during conversations. Maintaining proper eye contact shows attentiveness and respect; however, cultural differences exist regarding its interpretation.

Gestures: Hand movements and other gestures can emphasize points or replace verbal contact altogether. For example, giving a thumbs-up indicates approval without needing to say anything.

Proxemics: This refers to the use of personal space in conversation. Different cultures have different norms regarding physical proximity during conversations; understanding these can prevent discomfort or misunderstandings.

THE BEST WAY TO IMPROVE ON COMMUNICATION SKILLS

Haptics: Touch is another form of non-verbal communication that can convey support or aggression based on context and relationship dynamics.

Artifacts: These are objects that communicate messages about identity or status—such as clothing choices or accessories—that can influence how others view us.

Impact on Conversations

Statistics show that non-verbal cues account for up to 93% of communication effectiveness—55% through body language and facial emotions and 38% through tone of voice14. This means that only about 7% of our communication depends on the actual words we choose. Understanding this statistic shows the importance of being aware not only of what we say but also how we say it and how we present ourselves physically.

Non-verbal signals can support or contradict spoken words:

Reinforcement: When non-verbal cues align with verbal messages, they strengthen the overall connection. For example, saying "I'm excited" while smiling and using an enthusiastic tone improves the message's positivity.

Contradiction: Conversely, when non-verbal signals contradict verbal messages, confusion emerges. For instance, if someone says they are happy while pouting or avoiding eye contact, their body language suggests otherwise.

2.1 The Role Of Non-Verbal Communication In Relationships

Non-verbal communication is important for building and maintaining relationships:

Establishing Trust: Consistent non-verbal cues help create trust between individuals. When body language aligns with spoken words, it creates a sense of reliability and authenticity.

Enhancing Emotional Connection: Non-verbal signals help us to connect emotionally with others. A comforting touch or an encouraging nod can convey empathy and support that words alone might fail to explain.

Facilitating Understanding Across Cultures: Non-verbal communication transcends language boundaries. Gestures and expressions can often communicate meaning even when verbal communication fails due to language differences.

Practical Applications For Improving Non-Verbal Communication Skills

To harness the power of non-verbal communication successfully, consider the following practical strategies:

Be Mindful of Your Body Language: Pay attention to how your body language may be viewed by others. Practice keeping an open posture and using gestures that reinforce your spoken words.

Observe Others' Non-Verbal Cues: Enhance your observational skills by paying attention to the body language and face expressions of those around you. This will help you better understand their emotions and goals.

Practice Active Listening with Non-Verbal Engagement: When engaging in conversations, demonstrate active listening through your non-verbal cues—maintain eye contact, nod in agreement, and use suitable facial expressions to show empathy.

Adjust Your Tone Accordingly: Be aware of how your tone affects your message's reception. Practice varying your tone based on context—using

THE BEST WAY TO IMPROVE ON COMMUNICATION SKILLS

a warm tone for supportive talks or a firm tone for assertive discussions.

Seek Feedback: Ask trusted friends or colleagues for feedback on your non-verbal speaking skills. They may offer insights into how your body language affects their view during interactions.

The power of non-verbal communication cannot be underestimated; it plays a vital role in conveying feelings and intentions that words alone may not capture effectively. By understanding different types of non-verbal cues—such as body language, facial expressions, tone of voice, eye contact, gestures, proxemics, haptics, and artifacts—we can improve our ability to communicate effectively.

Recognizing the impact that non-verbal signals have on conversations helps us to become more intentional in our interactions with others. By practicing mindfulness regarding our non-verbal cues and developing observational skills to read those of others correctly, we can foster deeper connections and improve overall communication effectiveness.

Enhancing Communication Through Non-Verbal Skills

"The most important thing in communication is hearing what isn't said." – Peter Drucker. This quote stresses the critical role of non-verbal cues in understanding messages beyond words. Non-verbal communication includes various elements, including eye contact, posture, gestures, and facial expressions. Each of these components plays a significant role in conveying emotions and intentions, enhancing the total effectiveness of our interactions. In this chapter, we will study how to improve communication through non-verbal skills, focusing on eye contact, posture and gestures, and facial expressions.

THE BEST WAY TO IMPROVE ON COMMUNICATION SKILLS

Eye Contact

Eye contact is one of the most powerful kinds of non-verbal communication. It can create trust, convey interest, and display engagement during conversations. Here's how keeping appropriate eye contact can build rapport and enhance communication:

1. Establishing Trust

When you keep eye contact with someone during a conversation, it signals that you are present and fully engaged. This openness promotes trust between the speaker and the listener. Research suggests that people who make eye contact are perceived as more credible and trustworthy. This is particularly important in professional settings where establishing credibility can affect outcomes.

Practical Tip: Aim to keep eye contact for about 50-70% of the conversation. Too little eye contact may suggest disinterest or lack of confidence, while too much can feel threatening. Strive for a balance that feels comfortable.

2. Conveying Interest and Engagement

Eye contact helps express interest in what the other person is saying. It shows that you are actively listening and value their opinion. When you look someone in the eye while they talk, it encourages them to share more openly.

Practical Tip: Use "active listening" methods by nodding or using verbal affirmations like "I see" or "Go on" while keeping eye contact. This reinforces your involvement without interrupting their flow.

3. Navigating Cultural Differences

It's essential to understand that cultural norms regarding eye contact vary greatly. In some societies, direct eye contact is expected and seen as a sign of confidence; in others, it may be considered disrespectful or confrontational.

THE BEST WAY TO IMPROVE ON COMMUNICATION SKILLS

Practical Tip: Educate yourself about the cultural backgrounds of those you deal with to ensure your use of eye contact is appropriate and respectful.

Posture and Gestures

Posture and gestures are crucial aspects of body language that significantly impact how words are received in conversations.

1. Open Body Language

Adopting an open posture—where your arms are uncrossed, your body is facing the speaker, and your hands are visible—creates a welcoming atmosphere for conversation. Open body language signals receptiveness and encourages others to share their ideas without fear of judgment.

Practical Tip: Practice standing or sitting with an open posture during talks. Avoid crossing your arms or legs, as this can create a barrier between you and the speaker.

2. Gestures as Emphasis

Gestures can enhance verbal communication by emphasizing points or conveying emotions that words alone cannot describe. For example, using hand movements to illustrate an idea can make your message more engaging and memorable.

Practical Tip: Integrate natural gestures into your speech to stress key points. However, be careful not to overdo it; excessive gesturing can be distracting rather than helpful.

3. Mirroring

Mirroring includes subtly mimicking the other person's body language or gestures. This technique can build rapport and foster a sense of connection between individuals.

THE BEST WAY TO IMPROVE ON COMMUNICATION SKILLS

Practical Tip: If the person you're speaking with leans forward or uses specific gestures, try to mirror those actions slightly (without being obvious). This can improve feelings of empathy and understanding in the conversation.

Facial Expressions

Facial expressions are a basic component of non-verbal communication that communicates emotions and intentions effectively.

1. Conveying Empathy

Facial expressions play a crucial part in showing empathy during interactions. A genuine smile or a concerned look can express understanding and support without needing words.

Research Insight: Studies have shown that facial expressions associated with empathy—such as softening the eyes or slightly tilting the head—can significantly impact how others perceive our emotional involvement during conversations 12.

Practical Tip: Pay attention to your facial expressions while listening or reacting to someone's concerns. Practice softening your features when someone shares something emotional to express compassion effectively.

2. Recognizing Others' Emotions

Being able to read facial expressions helps us to respond appropriately to others' emotions. Recognizing signs of happiness, sadness, frustration, or confusion allows us to adjust our responses accordingly.

Practical Tip: Enhance your ability to read facial expressions by observing people in various contexts—whether in real life or through media—and practicing identifying their feelings based on their facial cues.

3. Matching Expressions

Matching your facial expressions to those of the speaker can build a sense of connection and understanding during conversations. This practice helps signal empathy and supports openness from both parties.

Practical Tip: If someone shares good news with excitement, reply with an enthusiastic smile; if they express sadness or frustration, adopt a concerned expression that reflects their feelings.

2.2 The Interplay Between Non-Verbal Cues

Understanding how eye contact, posture, gestures, and facial expressions work together improves our ability to communicate effectively:

Consistency Across Cues: Ensure that your non-verbal cues align with your verbal messages for maximum effect. For example, if you're expressing worry verbally but have closed-off body language (e.g., crossed arms), it may send mixed signals.

Feedback Loop: Non-verbal communication creates a feedback loop where each party's cues influence the other's reactions. For instance, if you maintain open body language while making eye contact, it encourages the speaker to connect more deeply with their message.

Cultural Sensitivity: As stated earlier, be aware that non-verbal cues can carry different meanings across cultures; what is considered positive body language in one culture might be read differently in another.

Enhancing communication through non-verbal skills is important for building trust, rapport, and deeper connections with others. By mastering eye contact, adopting open posture and gestures, and successfully using facial expressions, we can significantly improve our interactions both individually and professionally.

Practicing Non-Verbal Communication

In the realm of communication, non-verbal cues play a crucial part in how messages are conveyed and interpreted. As Peter Drucker aptly stated, "The most important thing in communication is hearing what isn't said." This chapter will explore practical exercises to enhance your non-verbal communication skills, provide scenarios for applying these skills in everyday interactions, and discuss the importance of cultural differences in interpreting non-verbal cues.

Engaging In Exercises To Practice Non-Verbal Skills

To improve your non-verbal communication, engaging in deliberate practice can be highly helpful. Here are several exercises intended to enhance your awareness and effectiveness in using non-verbal cues:

1. Mirror Exercise

Objective: To improve awareness of body language and facial expressions.

How to Do It: Pair up with a friend or family member. One person will talk about a topic of their choice while the other mirrors their body language and facial expressions as closely as possible. After a few minutes, switch places.

Benefits: This exercise helps you become more aware of how body language changes communication. It also allows you to see how your non-verbal signals can support or contradict your spoken words.

2. Emotion Charades

Objective: To practice conveying feelings through facial expressions and gestures.

THE BEST WAY TO IMPROVE ON COMMUNICATION SKILLS

How to Do It: Write down different feelings (e.g., happiness, sadness, anger, surprise) on slips of paper. Each participant takes turns drawing a slip and then uses only facial expressions and body language to convey the feeling to the group, who must guess what it is.

Benefits: This fun exercise improves your ability to express feelings without words and helps you recognize the subtle nuances of non-verbal communication.

3. Active Listening with Non-Verbal Cues

Objective: To improve active listening skills using non-verbal interaction.

How to Do It: During a conversation with someone, focus on using positive non-verbal cues—such as nodding, keeping eye contact, and leaning slightly forward—to show engagement. Afterward, discuss with the speaker how they felt during the chat.

Benefits: This exercise reinforces the importance of non-verbal signals in showing attentiveness and encourages deeper connections through effective listening.

4. Video Analysis

Objective: To analyze non-verbal communication in real-life situations.

How to Do It: Watch videos of speeches or chats (these could be TED Talks or interviews). Pay close attention to the speakers' body language, face expressions, and gestures. Take notes on how these elements add to their message.

Benefits: Analyzing others' non-verbal cues helps you understand their impact on communication effectiveness and offers insights into how you can improve your own delivery.

THE BEST WAY TO IMPROVE ON COMMUNICATION SKILLS

Scenarios For Applying Non-Verbal Skills

To truly enhance your ability to connect with others through non-verbal communication, it's essential to practice these skills in real-life situations. Here are some situations where you can practice:

1. Job Interview

In a job interview, your non-verbal communication can significantly influence the interviewer's impression of you.

Application: Maintain appropriate eye contact throughout the conversation to express confidence and interest. Sit up straight with an open stance, avoiding crossed arms or legs. Use hand gestures moderately to highlight key points when discussing your qualifications.

Outcome: By being aware of your non-verbal cues during the interview, you can create a positive impression that reinforces your verbal answers.

2. Conflict Resolution

During a dispute resolution discussion, successful non-verbal communication can help de-escalate tension.

Application: Use a calm tone of voice while keeping an open posture. Nod occasionally to show understanding and care. Avoid aggressive movements or facial expressions that could escalate the situation.

Outcome: By showing empathy through your body language and tone, you can foster a more constructive dialogue that leads to resolution rather than further conflict.

3. Social Gatherings

At social events or meetings, non-verbal skills can help you connect with new people.

Application: Approach others with an open stance and warm facial expression (e.g., smiling). Use proper eye contact while conversing to show interest in their stories. Lean slightly forward when listening to show engagement.

Outcome: These non-verbal signals can create a welcoming atmosphere that encourages others to open up and participate in meaningful conversations.

2.3 The Importance Of Cultural Differences In Interpreting Non-Verbal Cues

Understanding cultural differences is important when practicing non-verbal communication skills. Non-verbal cues can have vastly different meanings across cultures, which can lead to misunderstandings if not noticed.

1. Variability of Non-Verbal Cues

Different cultures have unique interpretations of different non-verbal signals:

Eye Contact: In many Western cultures, keeping eye contact is seen as a sign of confidence and honesty; however, in some Asian cultures, prolonged eye contact may be considered disrespectful or confrontational.

Gestures: A thumbs-up gesture may signify approval in some countries but could be offensive in others (e.g., parts of the Middle East). Similarly, personal space varies widely; some cultures are comfortable with close proximity during talks while others prefer more distance.

THE BEST WAY TO IMPROVE ON COMMUNICATION SKILLS

2. Contextual Understanding

Non-verbal communication is often contextual; understanding the cultural background of those you deal with enhances your ability to interpret their cues accurately:

Adaptability: Be willing to adjust your own non-verbal behaviors based on cultural norms when interacting with people from different backgrounds.

Awareness: Educate yourself about cultural differences related to body language, gestures, and proxemics (personal space) before participating in cross-cultural interactions.

Practicing non-verbal communication is important for enhancing interpersonal connections and improving overall communication efficiency. By participating in targeted exercises such as mirroring body language or analyzing emotional charades, individuals can develop greater awareness of their own non-verbal signals as well as those of others.

Applying these skills in real-life scenarios—such as job interviews or social gatherings—enables people to connect more deeply with others through effective use of eye contact, posture, gestures, and facial expressions.

Moreover, recognizing cultural differences in interpreting non-verbal cues is important for successful cross-cultural interactions. By being adaptable and aware of these differences, we can navigate diverse social landscapes more successfully.

As we continue our study of active listening throughout this book, remember that mastering non-verbal communication is a powerful tool for building deeper connections and enriching our interactions with others across all aspects of life.

THE BEST WAY TO IMPROVE ON COMMUNICATION SKILLS

CHAPTER THREE

3.0 Adapting Your Communication Style

"Communication works for those who work at it." – John Powell.

This quote underscores the effort needed to become an effective communicator by adapting styles to fit different audiences. In our increasingly diverse and interconnected world, the ability to recognize and change our communication styles is important for fostering understanding and building meaningful relationships. This chapter will cover different communication styles, strategies for identifying your style and recognizing others', and how adapting your style can lead to more productive conversations.

Recognizing Different Communication Styles

Understanding the different communication styles is essential to improving interpersonal relationships. While many frameworks exist, we can categorize

THE BEST WAY TO IMPROVE ON COMMUNICATION SKILLS

communication styles into four main types: assertive, passive, aggressive, and passive-aggressive. Each style has distinct characteristics that influence how people express themselves and interact with others.

1. Assertive Communication

Assertive communicators express their thoughts, feelings, and wants openly and honestly while respecting the rights of others. This style supports direct communication and encourages honest dialogue.

Characteristics:

Uses "I" sentences (e.g., "I feel..." or "I need...").

Maintains eye contact and an open stance.

Listens actively and respects differing views.

Effects on Interactions: Assertive communication promotes mutual respect, collaboration, and effective problem-solving. It helps individuals to express themselves without infringing on others' rights, leading to healthier relationships.

2. Passive Communication

Passive communicators often avoid expressing their thoughts or wants, prioritizing others' needs over their own. They may delay decision-making to avoid conflict.

Characteristics:

Avoids eye contact or shows closed body language.

Uses vague wording or agrees with others even when they disagree.

May show signs of anger or resentment over time.

Effects on Interactions: Passive speech can lead to misunderstandings, built-up anger, or resentment. It often results in unaddressed problems that can affect relationships negatively.

THE BEST WAY TO IMPROVE ON COMMUNICATION SKILLS

3. Aggressive Communication

Aggressive communicators prioritize their own wants above everyone else's, often disregarding others' rights in the process. They may dominate talks and belittle others.

Characteristics:

Uses loud tones or harsh words.

Displays intense eye contact that can be frightening.

Interrupts frequently and dismisses other views.

Effects on Interactions: Aggressive communication alienates others and can create a hostile atmosphere. While it may achieve quick results, it often harms relationships in the long run.

4. Passive-Aggressive Communication

Passive-aggressive communicators appear passive on the surface but show their anger indirectly through sarcasm or avoidance.

Characteristics:

Uses subtle hints or backhanded praise.

Engages in silent treatment or avoids conflict.

May show frustration through body language rather than words.

Effects on Interactions: This style causes confusion and tension in relationships as underlying issues stay unaddressed. It can lead to a loss of trust over time.

3.1 Strategies For Identifying Your Own Style

Recognizing your communication style is the first step toward successful adaptation:

Self-Reflection: Take time to reflect on how you typically communicate in different situations—

whether at work, home, or social settings. Consider whether you lean toward assertiveness, passivity, aggression, or passive-aggressiveness.

Feedback from Others: Ask trusted friends or colleagues for feedback about your conversation style. They can provide insights into how your method is perceived by others.

Journaling: Keep a journal of your interactions where you note your thoughts before and after conversations. This can help spot patterns in your communication style.

Recognizing Others' Styles For More Effective Engagement

Understanding the communication styles of those around you enhances your ability to connect effectively:

Observe Behavior: Pay attention to how individuals express themselves orally and non-verbally during conversations. Look for cues such as tone of voice, body language, and choice of words that suggest their style.

Ask Questions: Engage in open-ended questions that encourage others to share their thoughts and feelings more easily. For example, saying "How do you feel about this situation?" can reveal whether someone is assertive or more passive in their approach.

Practice Active Listening: Focus on understanding the speaker's message rather than preparing your response while they talk. This helps you to gauge their communication style based on their expressions and reactions during the conversation.

THE BEST WAY TO IMPROVE ON COMMUNICATION SKILLS

Adapting Your Style For Productive Conversations

Once you recognize both your communication style and that of others, adapting your method can lead to more productive conversations:

Flexibility: Be willing to adjust your communication style based on the context of the talk and the preferences of the other person involved. For example:

If speaking with a passive communicator, take a more assertive approach to encourage them to share their thoughts.

If engaging with an aggressive communicator, keep calmness and assertiveness while setting limits without escalating tensions.

Use Empathy: Show empathy by acknowledging the other person's feelings and opinions before expressing your views. This helps make a safe space for dialogue.

For instance, if someone shows frustration about a project at work, respond with understanding before sharing your thoughts on solutions.

Practice Assertiveness: Strive for assertiveness in most situations as it encourages healthy dialogue while respecting both parties' rights.

Use "I" statements to express your wants clearly (e.g., "I need more information before making a decision.").

Seek Common Ground: Look for areas of agreement during talks to build rapport with others regardless of their communication style.

If differences arise, frame them as opportunities for collaboration rather than conflict ("We have different perspectives; let's find a solution that works for both of us.").

THE BEST WAY TO IMPROVE ON COMMUNICATION SKILLS

Adapting your communication style is important for effective interaction in diverse settings—whether personal or professional. By recognizing different communication styles—assertive, passive, aggressive, and passive-aggressive—you can enhance your ability to engage successfully with others.

Identifying your style through self-reflection and feedback allows you to understand how you come across in talks while recognizing others' styles helps tailor your approach accordingly. By practicing flexibility, empathy, assertiveness, and seeking common ground during interactions, you open the way for more productive conversations that foster deeper connections.

Strategies For Tailoring Your Message

"Communication works for those who work at it." – John Powell. This quote highlights the effort needed to become an effective communicator, especially when it comes to adapting our messages to fit different audiences. Tailoring your message is important for ensuring that your communication resonates and inspires action. In this chapter, we will explore strategies for tailoring your message by knowing your audience, adjusting tone and language, and utilizing storytelling techniques.

1. Know Your Audience

Understanding your audience is the first step in tailoring your message successfully. By assessing their wants, preferences, and expectations, you can craft a message that speaks directly to them.

Techniques for Assessing Audience Needs

Conduct Research: Before engaging with your audience, gather information about their demographics, hobbies, and contact preferences. This could involve surveys, interviews, or analyzing current data.

THE BEST WAY TO IMPROVE ON COMMUNICATION SKILLS

Create Audience Personas: Develop detailed profiles of your target audience groups. These personas should include information about their goals, challenges, beliefs, and preferred communication styles. For example:

Persona 1: A young professional seeking job advancement who values concise and actionable advice.

Persona 2: A seasoned leader interested in strategic insights and long-term trends.

Engage in Active Listening: During conversations, practice active listening to understand your audience's views better. Ask open-ended questions to encourage dialogue and gain insights into their wants.

Observe Behavior: Pay attention to how your audience interacts with information across different platforms. Note what types of messages they engage with most—whether they prefer visual material, detailed reports, or quick summaries.

2. Adjusting Tone and Language

Once you have a clear idea of your audience, the next step is to adjust your tone and language based on the context—whether it's a formal or informal setting.

Modifying Language Based on Context

Formal vs. Informal Settings:

Formal Settings: In professional settings such as business meetings or presentations, use a more formal tone and precise language. Avoid colloquialisms or slang that may not connect with all audience members.

Example: Instead of saying "We need to get this done ASAP," you might say, "We must complete this task promptly."

THE BEST WAY TO IMPROVE ON COMMUNICATION SKILLS

Informal Settings: In casual talks or social gatherings, adopt a more relaxed tone that fosters connection. Use friendly language and relatable anecdotes to interest your audience.

Example: Instead of saying "This project has significant implications," you could say, "This project could change the game for us!"

Speak Their Language:

Tailor your message by using terminology familiar to your target. For example, if you're addressing a group of engineers, incorporate relevant technical jargon that they will understand while avoiding overly complicated language for a general audience.

Example: When talking a new software tool with tech-savvy colleagues, you might say, "This tool integrates seamlessly with our existing API," whereas with non-technical stakeholders you'd explain it as "This tool works well with our current systems."

Use Appropriate Visuals:

Incorporate visual aids such as graphs or infographics when presenting complicated information. Visuals can improve understanding and cater to different learning styles within your audience.

Ensure that visuals are clear and appropriate to the message being conveyed.

3. Using Storytelling

Storytelling is a powerful method in communication that can help engage, inform, and influence your audience like never before.

3.2 The Power Of Storytelling
Creating Emotional Connections:

Stories evoke emotions and build connections between the speaker and the audience. By sharing personal anecdotes or relatable situations, you can make your message more impactful.

Example: Instead of merely sharing statistics about a product's success, share a story about how it positively impacted a customer's life.

Simplifying Complex Ideas:

Storytelling can simplify complicated ideas by framing them within relatable narratives. This makes it easier for audiences to understand intricate ideas.

Example: When explaining a new process in your company, use a story about a team member who successfully navigated the process to illustrate its benefits.

Engaging Attention:

A well-crafted story captures attention and keeps the audience engaged throughout the presentation or chat.

Start with an intriguing hook or question connected to the story to draw listeners in from the beginning.

Providing Context:

Use storytelling to provide context for your message by showing real-world applications or consequences of an idea.

This contextualization helps audiences understand why the information is important to them personally.

Crafting Your Story

Identify Your Core Message:

Before crafting a story, clarify the core message you want to express. What do you want your listeners to learn or feel after hearing it?

Structure Your Story:

A compelling story typically follows a structure that includes an introduction (setting the scene), conflict

THE BEST WAY TO IMPROVE ON COMMUNICATION SKILLS

(the challenge faced), climax (the turning point), and conclusion (the outcome).

This structure helps keep interest and provides clarity.

Incorporate Relatable Characters:

Use characters in your stories that resonate with your audience's experiences or goals. This makes it easy for listeners to connect emotionally with the narrative.

Practice Delivery:

Rehearse telling your story until you feel comfortable with its flow and timing. Pay attention to non-verbal cues such as tone of voice and body language during delivery to improve engagement.

The Importance of Feedback

Tailoring your message is an ongoing process that benefits greatly from feedback:

Solicit Feedback from Your Audience:

After delivering a message or presentation, encourage comments from participants regarding clarity and engagement.

Use tools like surveys or informal talks to gather insights on how well your message resonated.

Adapt Based on Responses:

Be open to adjusting future communications based on feedback gained. If certain terms were confusing or if specific stories did not resonate as intended, modify them accordingly in future encounters.

Continuous Improvement:

View feedback as a chance for growth rather than criticism. Continuous improvement in communication skills improves effectiveness over time.

Adapting your communication style through tailored messaging is important for effective engagement

THE BEST WAY TO IMPROVE ON COMMUNICATION SKILLS

across different audiences. By knowing your audience—assessing their wants and preferences—you can craft messages that resonate deeply with them.

Adjusting tone and language based on context assures clarity while fostering connection; utilizing storytelling techniques allows you to engage emotions and simplify complicated ideas effectively.

Building Empathy Through Adaptation

"Communication works for those who work at it." – John Powell. This quote highlights the effort required to become an effective communicator, especially in adapting our styles to promote empathy and understanding. Building empathy through adaptation not only enhances mutual understanding but also strengthens relationships in both personal and professional settings. In this chapter, we will explore actionable techniques for encouraging empathy during conversations, provide real-life examples of successful outcomes through adaptive communication styles, and encourage readers to reflect on their experiences to identify areas for improvement.

Actionable Techniques For Fostering Empathy

Empathy is the ability to understand and share the thoughts of others. It is a crucial component of successful communication that can be cultivated through specific techniques:

1. Active Listening

Active listening is a basic skill for building empathy. It includes fully concentrating on what the speaker is saying, understanding their message, and responding thoughtfully.

Techniques:

Maintain Eye Contact: This shows the speaker that you are involved and interested in their message.

THE BEST WAY TO IMPROVE ON COMMUNICATION SKILLS

Use Verbal Affirmations: Phrases like "I understand" or "That makes sense" can motivate the speaker to continue sharing.

Paraphrase and Reflect: Summarize what the speaker has said to confirm your understanding and show that you are actively listening.

Example: During a talk with a friend who is going through a tough time, actively listen by nodding, keeping eye contact, and paraphrasing their feelings. For instance, you might say, "It sounds like you're feeling overwhelmed with everything happening at work."

2. Emotional Validation

Validating someone's feelings is important for fostering empathy. It includes acknowledging the emotions expressed by the speaker without judgment.

Techniques:

Acknowledge Feelings: Use words like "Understandably, you feel this way" or "I can see why you're upset."

Avoid Minimizing Their Experience: Refrain from saying things like "It's not that big of a deal" or "You'll get over it." Instead, focus on understanding their viewpoint.

Example: If a colleague shows frustration about a project delay, validate their feelings by saying, "I can see how disappointing that must be after all the hard work you've put in."

3. Adapt Your Communication Style

Tailoring your communication style to fit the needs of your audience can improve empathy. This includes recognizing different communication styles (assertive, passive, aggressive) and adjusting your method accordingly.

THE BEST WAY TO IMPROVE ON COMMUNICATION SKILLS

Techniques:

Identify Their Style: Observe how the other person communicates—are they straight, indirect, assertive, or passive? Adjust your style to match theirs where necessary.

Use Appropriate Language: Choose words that resonate with the other person's experiences and tastes.

Example: If you're discussing sensitive feedback with a team member who tends to be passive, approach them gently and use supportive language to make them feel safe sharing their thoughts.

Real-Life Examples of Successful Outcomes

Adapting communication styles can lead to successful outcomes in various situations, especially in conflict resolution and team collaboration.

Example 1: Conflict Resolution

In a workplace setting, two team members may have differing opinions on how to approach a project. One may prefer a more structured plan while the other likes flexibility.

Adaptation Strategy: The team leader sees these differing styles and facilitates a discussion where both views are validated. By using active listening techniques and encouraging each member to share their thoughts fully without interruption, the leader creates an atmosphere of respect.

Outcome: By adapting her communication style to foster open dialogue, the leader helps the team find common ground—combining structure with flexibility—resulting in a cohesive plan that satisfies both sides.

THE BEST WAY TO IMPROVE ON COMMUNICATION SKILLS

Example 2: Team Collaboration

During a brainstorming session, one team member tries to dominate discussions while others stay silent.

Adaptation Strategy: The facilitator notices this dynamic and consciously adapts her approach by directly asking quieter members to share their ideas. She uses open body language and keeps eye contact with each participant as she encourages contributions from everyone.

Outcome: By adapting her facilitation style to ensure inclusivity, she fosters an environment where all opinions are heard. This leads to more diverse ideas being generated and eventually enhances team creativity.

Reflecting on Personal Experiences

Encouraging readers to reflect on their experiences can help find areas for change in adaptability:

Self-Assessment:

Encourage readers to think about past talks where they struggled to connect with others. What conversation style did they use? Were they aware of the other person's style?

Ask them to consider how adapting their approach could have changed the result of those interactions.

Journaling Reflections:

Suggest keeping a journal where they record instances of successful empathetic communication as well as times when they felt disconnected from others.

Prompt them to analyze what worked well in successful exchanges and what could be improved in less effective ones.

Setting Goals for Improvement:

THE BEST WAY TO IMPROVE ON COMMUNICATION SKILLS

Encourage readers to set specific goals for enhancing their adaptability in future talks. This could include practicing active listening methods or consciously adjusting their tone based on context.

Suggest they seek feedback from friends or colleagues about their speaking style and areas for growth.

Building empathy through adaptation is important for enhancing mutual understanding in all kinds of interactions. By equipping oneself with actionable methods such as active listening, emotional validation, and adapting communication styles, individuals can create deeper connections with others.

Real-life examples show how adapting communication styles can lead to successful outcomes in conflict resolution and team collaboration. Encouraging reflection on personal experiences allows readers to spot areas for improvement in their adaptability.

THE BEST WAY TO IMPROVE ON COMMUNICATION SKILLS

CONCLUSION

As we conclude our exploration of effective communication skills in "The Best Way to Improve on Communication Skills: Unlock the Secrets of Active Listening for Deeper Connections," it is essential to reflect on the key takeaways from each chapter. Active listening stands as a cornerstone of effective communication, enabling us to build deeper connections, foster empathy, and navigate complex interactions with greater ease.

The Foundation of Active Listening:

Active listening is defined as a conscious effort to engage fully with the speaker, understand their message and respond thoughtfully. This chapter emphasized the importance of being fully present, using positive body language, and paraphrasing or reflecting on what is said. By mastering these techniques, we can enhance our ability to connect with others and reduce misunderstandings.

THE BEST WAY TO IMPROVE ON COMMUNICATION SKILLS

The Power of Non-Verbal Communication:

Non-verbal cues—such as eye contact, posture, gestures, and facial expressions—play a critical role in communication. Research indicates that up to 93% of communication effectiveness comes from non-verbal signals. Understanding and effectively using these cues can reinforce our messages and help us convey empathy and understanding.

Practicing Non-Verbal Communication:

Engaging in exercises to improve non-verbal skills can significantly enhance our interactions. By applying techniques such as mirroring body language or analyzing emotional responses in conversations, we can become more attuned to both our own signals and those of others. Additionally, recognizing cultural differences in non-verbal communication is crucial for effective cross-cultural interactions.

NICK EVANS BROWN

Adapting Your Communication Style:

Recognizing different communication styles (assertive, passive, aggressive) enables us to adapt our approach based on the context and audience. By identifying our style and observing others', we can tailor our messages for greater impact. This adaptability fosters more productive conversations and helps resolve conflicts effectively.

Building Empathy Through Adaptation:

Fostering empathy during conversations enhances mutual understanding. Techniques such as active listening, emotional validation, and adapting communication styles contribute to creating a supportive environment where individuals feel heard and respected. Real-life examples illustrate how adaptive communication leads to successful outcomes in conflict resolution and team collaboration.

THE BEST WAY TO IMPROVE ON COMMUNICATION SKILLS

Strategies for Tailoring Your Message:

Understanding your audience's needs and preferences is essential for effective communication. By adjusting tone and language based on context—whether formal or informal—and utilizing storytelling techniques, we can engage our audience more deeply and inspire action.

Implementing Techniques in Daily Interactions

As you move forward from this book, I encourage you to implement the techniques learned consistently in your daily interactions:

Practice Active Listening: Make it a habit to fully engage in conversations by maintaining eye contact, using positive body language, and paraphrasing what you hear. Set listening goals before meetings or discussions to remind yourself to focus on understanding rather than responding.

Be Mindful of Non-Verbal Cues: Pay attention to your non-verbal signals as well as those of others. Practice using open body language and appropriate facial expressions to convey empathy and engagement.

Adapt Your Communication Style: Reflect on your communication style in various contexts. Consider how you can adjust your approach based on the needs of your audience or the situation at hand.

Utilize Storytelling: Incorporate storytelling into your communications to make your messages more relatable and memorable. Share personal anecdotes or relevant examples that resonate with your audience's experiences.

Inspiring Ongoing Growth

Mastering communication skills is an ongoing journey that requires practice, reflection, and a willingness to learn from experiences. Here are some suggestions for further developing your skills:

THE BEST WAY TO IMPROVE ON COMMUNICATION SKILLS

Seek Feedback: After conversations or presentations, ask trusted friends or colleagues for feedback on your communication style. Inquire about areas where you excelled as well as aspects that could be improved.

Engage in Continuous Learning: Explore additional resources such as books, online courses, or workshops focused on communication skills and active listening techniques. Engaging with diverse materials can provide new insights and strategies.

Reflect Regularly: At the end of each day or week, take time to reflect on your interactions. Consider what went well and what challenges you faced in communicating effectively. Use these reflections to set goals for improvement moving forward.

Practice Mindfulness: Incorporate mindfulness practices into your daily routine to enhance your ability to stay present during conversations.

Techniques such as mindful breathing or meditation can help you cultivate awareness and focus.

Join a Group or Community: Participate in groups focused on improving communication skills—such as Toastmasters or local discussion clubs—where you can practice speaking and listening in a supportive environment.

Final Thoughts

Effective communication is not just about exchanging information; it is about building relationships, fostering understanding, and connecting with others on a deeper level. By embracing the principles of active listening outlined in this book and committing to continuous improvement, you will not only enhance your communication skills but also contribute positively to the interactions you have with others.

Remember that mastery comes with practice and reflection; every conversation is an opportunity for

THE BEST WAY TO IMPROVE ON COMMUNICATION SKILLS

growth. As you apply these techniques in your daily life, you will find yourself better equipped to navigate complex social landscapes with confidence, empathy, and effectiveness.

Thank you for embarking on this journey toward improving your communication skills! May you unlock the secrets of active listening for deeper connections that enrich both your personal life and professional endeavors.

Thank you so much for making it to the end of the book!

I truly appreciate the time you've taken to read my work. As an independent Kindle publisher, your support means everything to me. I hope you've found valuable and useful insights in these pages.

If you could spare just 60 seconds, I'd love to hear your honest feedback on Amazon. Your feedback makes a huge difference and it does wonders for the book. I also enjoy hearing about your experiences with it!

To leave your feedback, simply copy the link below and paste it into your browser:

www.ingramcontent.com/pod-product-compliance
Lightning Source LLC
Chambersburg PA
CBHW071050240526
45469CB00006BD/2293